Foreword

Zolushka's New Life

Nearly a decade ago, in 2008, the Russian Academy of Sciences (RAS) established a project, the "Special Permanent Expedition of RAS," to study endangered Russian wildlife. Under the auspices of this Permanent Expedition, and with support from the Russian Geographical Society, the A.N. Severtsov Institute of Ecology and Evolution (part of RAS) launched an ambitious, multi-faceted scientific program to study Amur tigers.

Our goal is to restore their populations in the Russian Far East. We've used the most modern methods in this work: satellite collars to study the movements of wild tigers, molecular genetic diagnostics to determine kinship among individuals, hormone analysis to remotely understand the physical condition of wild animals, and a study of infectious diseases.

Importantly, we have also identified places in the Far East where tigers used to roam, but are absent now due to human pressures, and where they could thrive once again.

In the process of our work we kept encountering tiger cubs — young animals orphaned in the wild by poachers. These unfortunate animals were often exhausted and frost-bitten, and had no enviable future. We decided to help. Along with Inspection Tiger we built a rehabilitation center near the village of Alekseevka and started bringing orphaned cubs there. We hoped that, if raised properly in captivity, these cubs could be released back into the wild once they were old enough to fend for themselves. We decided that release sites should not be where there are Amur tigers today, but where they once were and disappeared because of humans.

Many of my colleagues took part in this effort. We wanted to minimize contact between the cubs and humans, so we installed remote-controlled cameras in large, open-air cages. The cubs had to learn how to hunt their natural prey — deer and wild boar — on their own. They had to learn how to properly act around other tigers and how to avoid confrontations with humans. In the process, we developed a special and effective system for rehabilitating tiger cubs and preparing them for a return to the wild.

Zolushka was found in the forest, half dead, and brought to the rehabilitation center. We had to amputate the tip of her frost-bitten tail, but then we largely let her be. Zolushka began to recover. We spent about a year and a half preparing for her release. During this time it was almost like Zolushka was in school — learning to be a tiger all on her own, and she had to pass specific "exams" before she could "graduate." Zolushka excelled in the ability to hunt, on how to interact with other tigers, and how to avoid humans, thus passing all her tests with flying colors. Then, equipped with a satellite collar, she was brought to Bastak Reserve in the Pri-Amur Region and released.

Fortunately, Zolushka thrived in her new home.

The Pri-Amur was, for decades, a region without tigers. Now these forests are also home to other tigers we have saved. Thus, with this project we are not only saving the lives of cubs otherwise certain to die, but we are also creating a group of founders that will restore tiger populations where they were once lost.

Prof. Viatcheslav V. Rozhnov

Director, A.N. Severtsov Institute of Ecology and Evolution, Russian Academy of Sciences, and Chief of the Permanent Expedition of RAS for the study of Russian Red Book animals and other key animals of Russian fauna

Hello. I am Zolushka.

In English, my name means Cinderella.
So basically, I am a princess.

I am an Amur tiger, otherwise known as a Siberian tiger.
We are one of the biggest tigers in the world.

I live in the Russian Far East, in a big dense forest that has everything that I need. I hunt for elk, wild boar, sika deer, badgers and even, occasionally, a brown bear.

6

To learn about a tiger, you have to ask a tiger. We are carnivorous. That means we only eat meat. No plants ever. We need to be fast, so we can catch the things we eat.

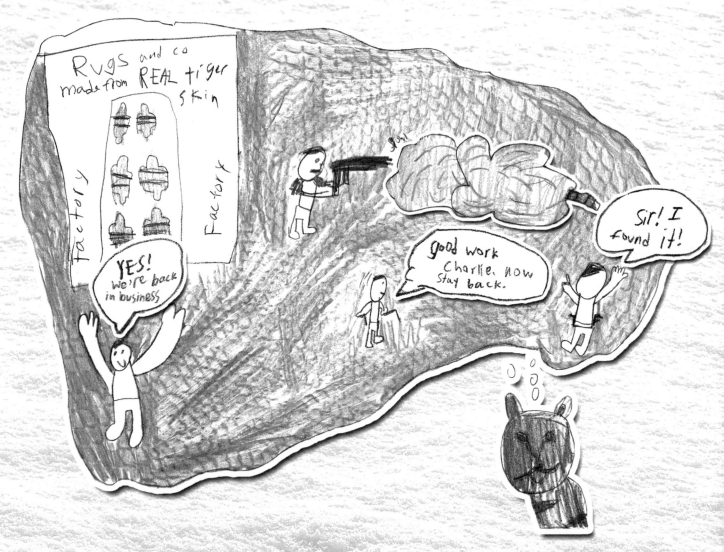

While we tigers are gorgeous and really cool — no two tigers' stripes are the same — we are not perfectly safe. Some people think we are great rugs. Can you believe them? These people are called poachers. They hunt us for our beautiful fur. There used to be no rules about killing us.

Our home was also being divided into patches. Loggers
would come in, chop down trees and cart them away.
Prey became scarce. Roads also led the poachers to us.

Here is a devastating fact. There are only six out of nine tiger sub-species left on earth: Bengal tigers, South-China tigers, Indo-China tigers, Malayan tigers, Sumatran tigers and me.

The Bali tiger, Javan tiger and Caspian tiger are all extinct. That means there are no more of them left.

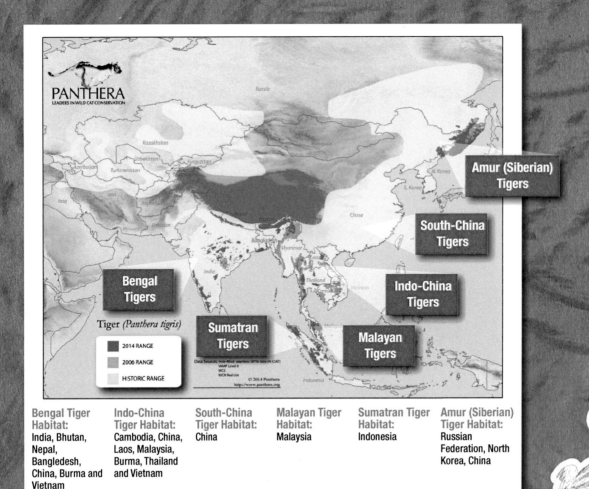

Bengal Tiger Habitat: India, Bhutan, Nepal, Bangledesh, China, Burma and Vietnam

Indo-China Tiger Habitat: Cambodia, China, Laos, Malaysia, Burma, Thailand and Vietnam

South-China Tiger Habitat: China

Malayan Tiger Habitat: Malaysia

Sumatran Tiger Habitat: Indonesia

Amur (Siberian) Tiger Habitat: Russian Federation, North Korea, China

oh No!

I'm sad to say, I'm one of only 3,500 or so tigers left on earth. I am always wondering, will I be next?

Today, there are about 500 Amur tigers in the wild. You can help to make sure I live.

My mom and I used to travel a lot.
We always found a nice place to
sleep, in a den or a cozy cave.

We rarely ran into other tigers, but when we did, mom would stand her ground and let out a horrible ear-splitting roar. I always felt safe with her around.

When I was really young, she would go hunting
and come back with deer or wild boar. My mom
could eat around 60 pounds of meat.

Sometimes she would catch a rabbit or fish,
just for me.

I remember her letting me eat first.
I remember snuggling up with my mom at night,
her warm coat protecting me.

One day we were out hunting. I heard the birds
chirping and the snow shining like silver outside.

All of a sudden, we heard voices. "Hide!" My mother called out. I heard a crack and a thump as something heavy fell to the ground. I ran away as fast as my legs would carry me.

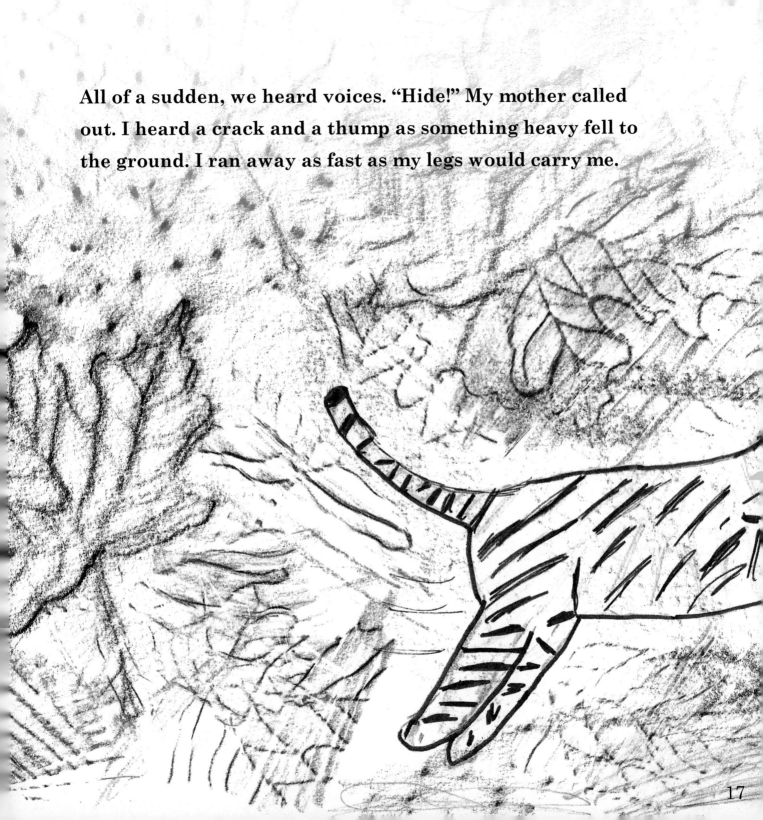

It was so cold and so windy. "Mama!" I called out.
But she was nowhere to be seen. I shivered. It was
getting colder, and my tail was getting numb.

I held onto hope, hope to see my mom again, hope to be happy. Then everything started to get blurry, and I felt my eyes starting to close.

My hope of surviving the winter vanished. I lay down in the cold and brutal drift of snow, ready to die. My tail was dead.

I woke up later from the rustling in the trees.
The sound kept getting closer and closer.
Then I saw them. And they saw me.

They started slowly approaching me. I wanted to run or
growl, but couldn't. I was too weak to move. I needed food
and water, but to get those things I needed my mother.
I wanted to cry out, but was in too much pain.

Then big strong arms wrapped around me. They threw a blanket over me. It was dark, and I couldn't see.

They lifted me up off the ground. I was scared. I didn't know why or where I was going. Everything was a blur of pain.

Andre Oryol, the wildlife inspector to whom Zolushka was first taken.

Next thing I knew, I was sitting in a dark shed in a soft pile of hay. The humans slowly lifted the cloth off my head. I looked around, then shivered. This place was not my home.

They fed me eggs, raw meat and nice warm milk.
In two weeks, I was back on my four paws.

Then a man took a long needle and pressed it firmly
into my skin. I fell asleep.

When I awoke, the frost-bitten part of my tail was gone. It had been cut clean off.

Then I knew they weren't going to kill me. In fact, they were saving me. They called me "Zolushka."

At first, in my enclosure, there were only pieces of meat for me to eat, but as time went by there were these fast, small animals that I had to chase. I saw a little furball, and I realized it was a rabbit.

I was unsure of what to do, but then I started to get really, really hungry. I eventually found out that I could eat the rabbit. So I pounced. And boy, was it delicious.

After a while, they put me in a little forest.

I got the hang of killing these strange animals. For once in a long time, I was actually proud of myself.

It felt like my mother was right by my side, helping as I went on.

The animals kept getting bigger and bigger. Soon, there was a big tasty tusked animal for me to devour.

I hid in the grass, lay in the sun and hid my kill.

One thing increased. My hunger. Hunger for bravery. This place was and is my new home.

One day, I felt a sharp pain, and then I got really
sleepy. I blacked out. I woke up to find myself in a
small, dark box with something around my neck.

I heard voices coming from outside the box.
I lay down and sighed. I wished I were back home.

31

Suddenly, the box started moving. The ground seemed to shake beneath me. I started panicking. Why am I here? Am I moving? Are they taking me to my mom? So many questions.

For the first time in so long, I wanted to be
small again. I wanted mama to bring me
food at night. I just wanted my mama.

I peered through the crack of my cage and saw wilderness.
Then the truck came to a halt. I heard footsteps.

Soon, I heard a rumble. The doors started opening.
All I could see was the endless expanse of trees.

I stared around for a few seconds until I realized, I was free!

I leaped, hay scattered everywhere, wind smacked my face. I started running. I didn't know where I was running, and I didn't care.

Look out world, here comes Zolushka!
Just like that, I was alone in the thick, dense forest.

I kept on bounding farther into the woods.

I was the first tiger cub ever to be rehabilitated and then released as an adult back into the wild in Russia.

I was so surprised how many animals were there. And here's the best thing: they all tasted different.

Wherever I went I looked for the boxes — cameras. They let scientists and the whole world know about me: where I live, what I look like, and most importantly, my life story.

Somewhere out there, everyone who had helped was still watching me from far away.

Then one beautiful sunny day, I was on my morning stroll when I saw something in the bushes. At first, I thought it was a boar, but then the most beautiful tiger I had ever seen stepped towards me.

It was love at first sight. Soon, my mate Zavetny was always by my side. Before I knew it, I was pregnant.

I got tired. Three-and-a-half months later, I felt stabs of pain, then I felt a "pop." My body started feeling lighter as I saw the two little tigers lying in a small heap. They were beautiful.

I am a mom! Never have I experienced so much love and joy.

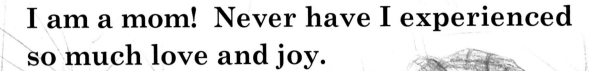

The cubs wrestle, sending up snow into the frosty air, and climb all over me.

They are a lot of work. I have to care for them, wash them, protect them, feed them, teach them how to hunt and what to eat.

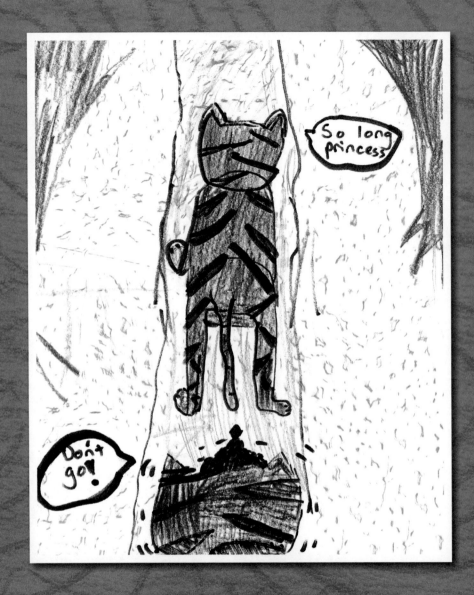

By then, Zavetny had run off. "Why are you leaving me?"
I asked. He said, "It's my instinct at this time."

You could see his shadow running farther and farther away.

I wake up to the sound of the birds.

I always lean over to check that my cubs are there. Then I gracefully leap over them and set off for my hunt. When I am done, I come home to find my hungry cubs waiting. Then we all sit down to feast on the delightful meal I caught.

I am like the mother I barely had. I'm back. I'm strong and healthy. I have two cubs. I'm in the wild.

It may seem like my battle was won. But it's not.
This is just the beginning.

Tigers are still being hunted down, killed.

My human helpers changed me from a sick tiger, who was afraid and near death, to a healthy one. They taught me to hunt.

They understood that I needed love and kindness to get better. People are rehabilitating and tracking us and catching poachers, so that we will remain wild and free.

I look out into the beautiful mountains. My cubs wake up, and I point out tons of animals and plants that live here. I used to be one of the only tigers here, but now there are more of us.

The place I live is so special, and I would love to stay forever.

The world would be a sad, sad place without us.

I give a big thanks to you, reader.

I know you'll help me and make a big difference.

Simple Ways To Help

- Buy only 100-percent recycled toilet paper and tissues that aren't made of our trees.

- Look for Rain-Forest Alliance certified coffee.

- Buy only RSPO (Roundtable on Sustainable Palm Oil-certified) oil.

- Make pine-nut free pesto. (People destroy our homes to get pine nuts.)

- Only buy wood certified by the Forest Stewardship Council (FSC), so it doesn't come from our forests.

- Spread the word. Tell your family, friends, teachers — and even strangers — about us and how they can help.

Afterword

Zolushka.

The story told by the class of P.S. 107 is one of bravery and survival. When found by a band of hunters, nearly unconscious from cold and hunger, Zolushka likely had only hours left to live. Yet, she did not give up, and neither did these people who found themselves entrusted with her fate. Amazingly, these warm-hearted hunters gave up their expedition to spend that day carrying Zolushka and then driving her to the nearest wildlife inspector.

Given that another hunter-turned-poacher was likely responsible for killing Zolushka's mother and putting her in this life-and-death predicament, this unlikely act of kindness from these roughshod hunters was an odd twist of fate. From this point onwards, a series of heroic actions by a broad range of people eventually gave Zolushka a second chance at life in the wilds of the Russian Far East: from the hunters who first picked her up; to the wildlife inspector who first took care of her; to the veterinarians who oversaw her development and prepared her return to the wild; to the people of Bastak Reserve, who welcomed her; to Director Rozhnov of the Severtsov Institute in Moscow, who conceived of the Rehabilitation Center where Zolushka was kept and oversaw her release. All these people committed small and large acts of courage, putting the welfare of this little cub (and then not-so-little teenage tigress) above their own interests.

Zolushka not only survived, but thrived in her new home, and ultimately demonstrated her complete return to the wild when she appeared before camera traps with two young cubs. Such cubs are so rarely captured before camera traps that it seemed as if Zolushka had decided to parade her new family before the cameras, as if to say "thank you" to all her benefactors.

Perhaps more importantly, this story is about another kind of survival — that of an entire species. Zolushka has shown us that it is possible to reintroduce young cubs into areas that have lost their tigers. Unfortunately, such places are common across the tiger's former range in Asia today — extensive forests that once held tigers now echo with a sad emptiness rather than the roar of the "jungle king." But Zolushka's tale tells us that it is possible to return tigers to these forests — as long as enough suitable prey exist and protection is provided. Thus Zolushka's tale of survival provides a roadmap for survival of the species.

Finally, this is the story of survival of the human spirit. Uncommon acts of kindness, bravery, and self-sacrifice were necessary for this "fairy tale" to come true. Without cooperation among multiple people and organizations — both Russian and international — a happy ending would have been impossible. Thanks to the children of P.S. 107, who decided to tell this story, there is now an opportunity for more people to learn about Zoluskha. That so many people from those first hunters to the kids of P.S. 107 came together to provide a future for this single tigress gives me hope —not only for Zolushka and all tigers but for us humans as well. With concerted cooperation, a touch of kindness, and unadulterated bravery, perhaps we can find a balance and a future living here on Mother Earth.

Dale Miquelle
Director of the Russia Program
Wildlife Conservation Society

Beast Relief, a PTA committee at P.S. 107, teaches children about the need for conservation, instills in them a love of animals and takes concrete steps to help animals far and near. Every year, in partnership with a wildlife organization, our fifth graders write and illustrate a book about a real endangered animal. All proceeds from the self-published books, which are available for purchase on Amazon.com, go directly to the wildlife organizations. *One Special Tiger* is the fourth book in our One Special Animal series. Also available:

One Special Rhino
The Story of Andatu
Written and illustrated by the fifth graders of P.S. 107 John W. Kimball Learning Center
with foreword by Dr. Jane Goodall

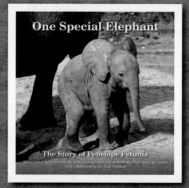

One Special Elephant
The Story of Penelope Petunia
Written and illustrated by the fifth graders of P.S. 107 John W. Kimball Learning Center
with a foreword by Dr. Jane Goodall

One Special Orangutan
The Story of Budi
Written and illustrated by the fifth graders of P.S. 107 John W. Kimball Learning Center

Acknowledgements

The P.S. 107 Beast Relief committee would like to thank the following individuals and organizations for their support.

In Russia, many people helped Zolushka survive. Prof. Viatcheslav V. Rozhnov, Director of the A.N. Severtsov Institute of Ecology and Evolution started the Alekseevka Rehabilitation Center, and oversaw the translocation of Zolushka to her new home. He provided the book's foreword.

The staff of the Severtsov Institute include: Sergei Naidenko, Pavel Sorokin, José-Antonio Hernandez-Blanco, Anna Yachmennikova, Maria Chistopolova, Natalia Esaulova, Andrei Kotlyar and Mikhail Litvinov. Ekaterina Blidchenko helped care for all the tigers that have been rehabilitated at Alekseevka.

Victor Gaponov managed the Alekseevka center while Zolushka was there. Financial support for Zolushka's care came from the Russian Geographical Society, Phoenix Fund, and the International Fund for Animal Welfare. Mikhail Alshenitskii of the Moscow Zoo, Irina Korotkova and Galina Ivanchuk of the Primorskii Agricultural Academy offered veterinary care for Zolushka. Ivan and Olga Polkovnikov monitor Zolushka in the Bastak Reserve. Aleksandr Y. Kalinin, the Bastak Reserve director, took responsibility for releasing Zolushka into his reserve. Viktor Kuzmenko, director of the PRNCO Tiger Centre, also aided these efforts.

The Wildlife Conservation Society partnered with the P.S. 107 Beast Relief committee on this book. Nat Moss, WCS' senior writer, introduced us to WCS' Russia and Northeast Asia Coordinator Jonathan C. Slaght, Ph.D. Throughout this project, Dr. Slaght served as our expert advisor and led an assembly that taught the fifth graders about Amur tigers. In Russia, at the children's request, he filmed interviews with Sasha Rybin, Field Specialist, and Dr. Dale Miquelle, Director of the WCS Russia Program. Dr. Miquelle, one of the world's foremost Siberian tiger experts, provided the book's afterword. Inside WCS, Kathi Schaeffer, Executive Director of Public Affairs and Partnerships, helped guide the book project.

At P.S. 107, Eve Litwack, our principal, championed this project and provided essential logistical support, as did parent coordinator Heather Damon. Fifth-grade teachers Ed Schulz, Michael Carlson and Shirley Harkins helped bring this project to all 95 fifth graders. All the illustrations and words in this book are their own. Beast Relief also acknowledges the work of its book committee. Members include: Mariko Beck, Kajal Below, Katherine Eban, Spring Hofeldt, Mary Huhn, Maureen McLaughlin, Grace Sharfstein, Tracy Tullis and Julie Brunner Cross, the school's art teacher, who helped develop the artwork.

Fifth Grade Authors and Illustrators

Emily Olive
Sakura Aster
Tara Scott Zach
Noah Isaac Boaz
Emma Lily Abby
Olga Una Ellie
Sofia Eva
Gus

Chase Lucy Ali
Zelda Mia Yuki
Alexander Lucy
Lindsey Erik
Aila Eva Mia
Dory Maya

Gisele
Terefech Ines
Takumi Sadie
Natalie Audrey
Emerson Alexander
Noah Marlee Daniel
Siahvash Simon
Kamilo Anya
Meital

Ava
River JAKE
Paloma Kiera
Sofia Reuben
Carter Audrey
Shelby Sophie
Rosemary
Grace

LEONIE Lena
Stella Talia Elan
Orli Dafna Maya Daniel
Chelsea Sienna Heather Ruby
Amelia Emerson Alex Kiran Avi
Hannah Jesse Carolina Hazel
Jess Alex Dino Wilson Aaron
Malachi Cerys Delia Alex

53